Dr. Kanner, Dentist with a Smile

written by
ALICE K. FLANAGAN

photographs by
CHRISTINE OSINSKI

Reading Consultant
LINDA CORNWELL
Learning Resource Consultant
Indiana Department of Education

CHILDREN'S PRESS®   *A Division of Grolier Publishing*
New York • London • Hong Kong • Sydney • Danbury, Connecticut

Special thanks to Joshua Kanner for allowing us to tell his story.

Library of Congress Cataloging-in-Publication Data
Flanagan, Alice.
    Dr. Kanner, dentist with a smile / written by Alice K. Flanagan ; photographs by Christine Osinski ; reading consultant, Linda Cornwell.
        p. cm. — (Our neighborhood)
    Summary: Introduces the dentist and explains his work in cleaning and caring for the teeth of his patients.
    ISBN 0-516-20493-9 (lib.bdg.)   0-516-26210-6 (pbk.)
    1. Dentists—Juvenile literature. [1. Dentists. 2. Dental care. 3. Occupations.] I. Osinski, Christine, ill. II. Title. III. Series: Our neighborhood.
RK63.F53 1997
617.6—dc21   97-4137
                                               CIP
                                               AC

Photographs ©: Christine Osinski

Down the street in a red brick house is Dr. Kanner's office.

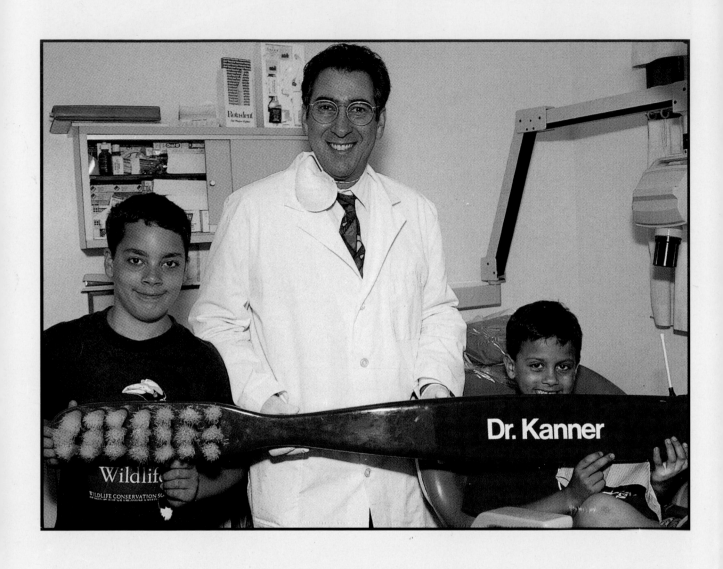

Dr. Kanner is our family dentist.
He takes care of our teeth and
makes sure our mouths stay healthy.

When things get busy at the office, another dentist helps him.

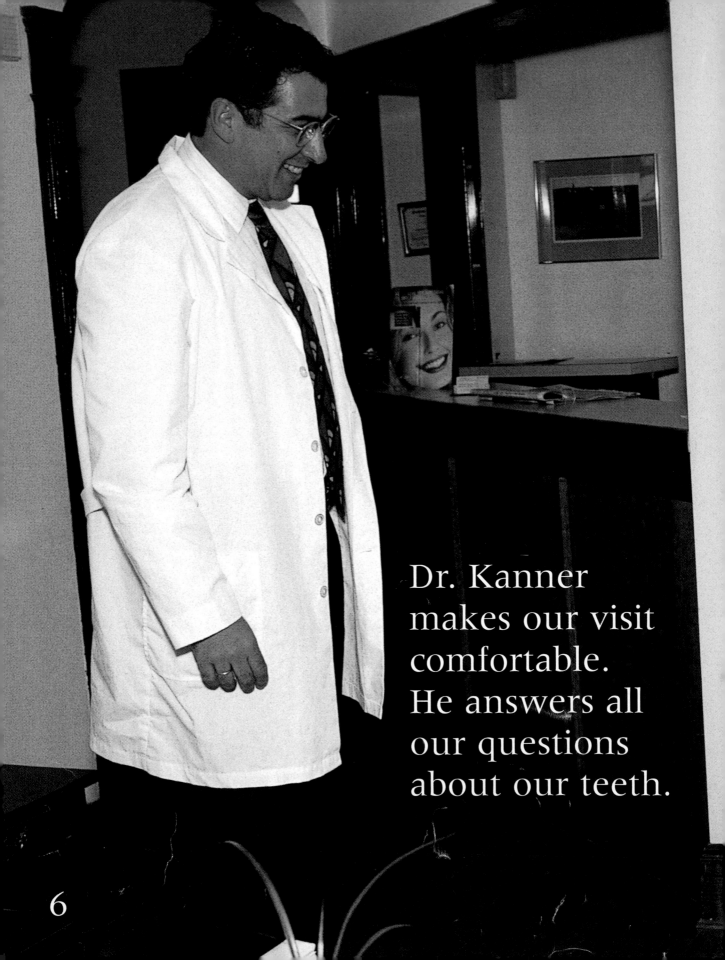

Dr. Kanner makes our visit comfortable. He answers all our questions about our teeth.

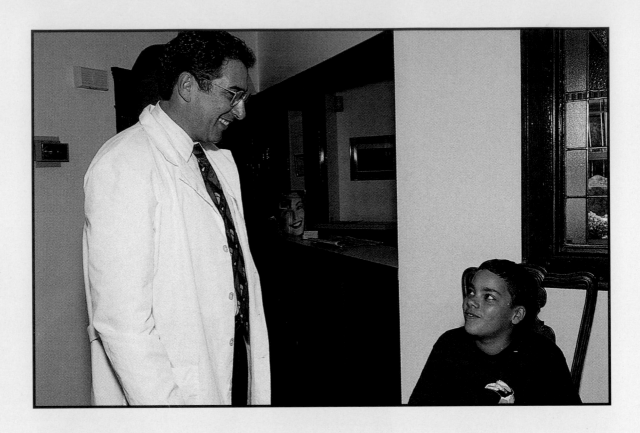

He helps children and adults.

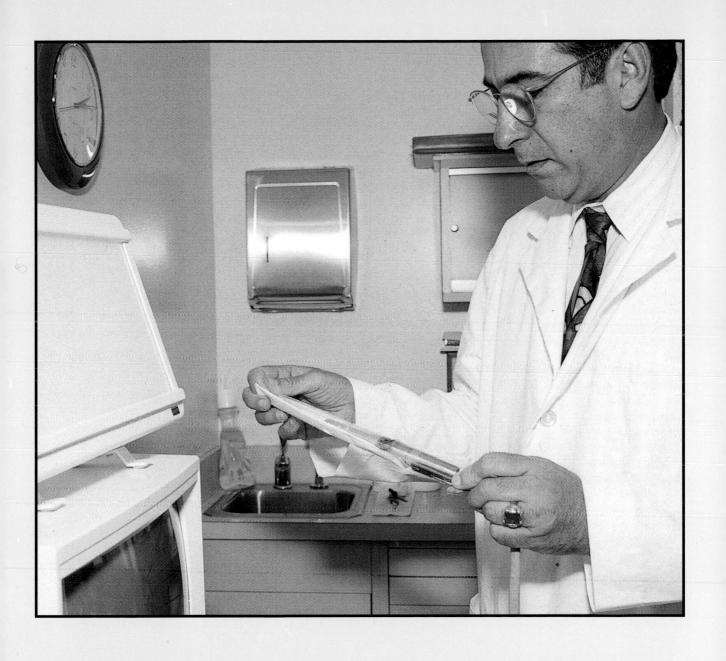

In his office, everything is clean and free of germs.

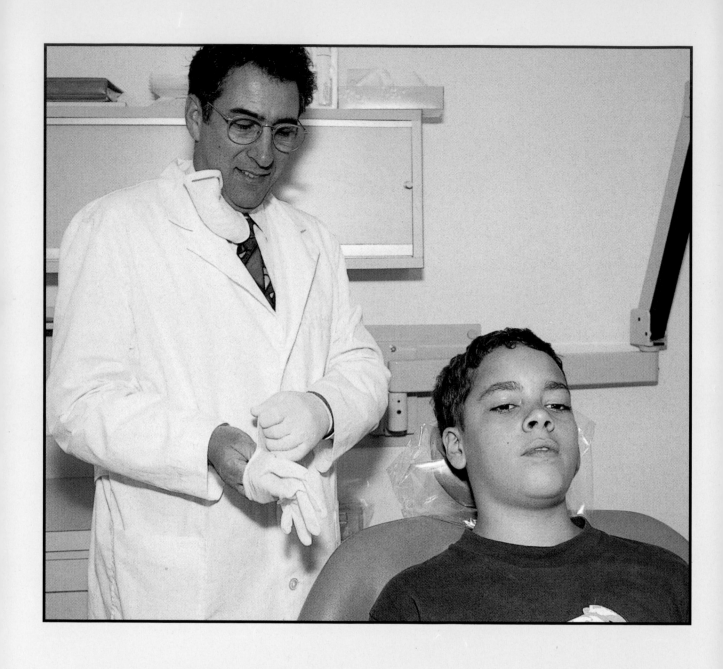

Dr. Kanner wears a mask and covers his hands with soft, rubber gloves.

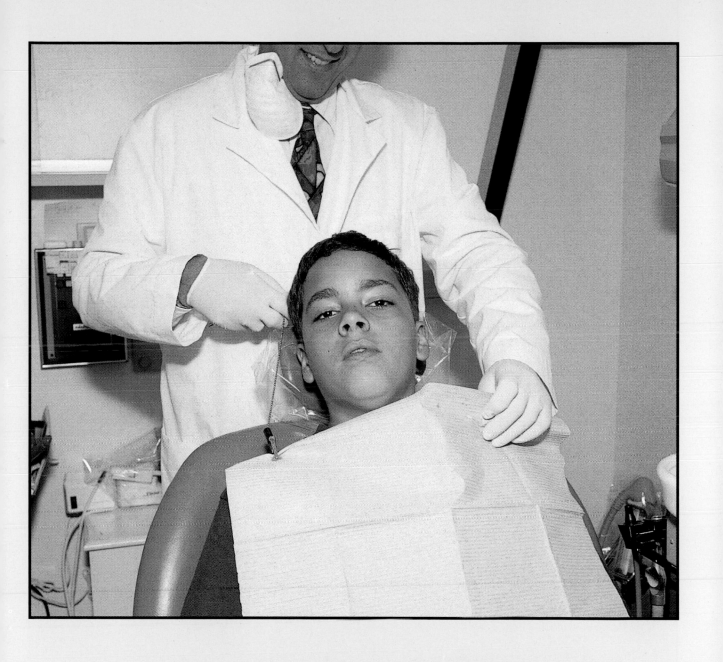

He puts a fresh paper bib on us to protect our clothes.

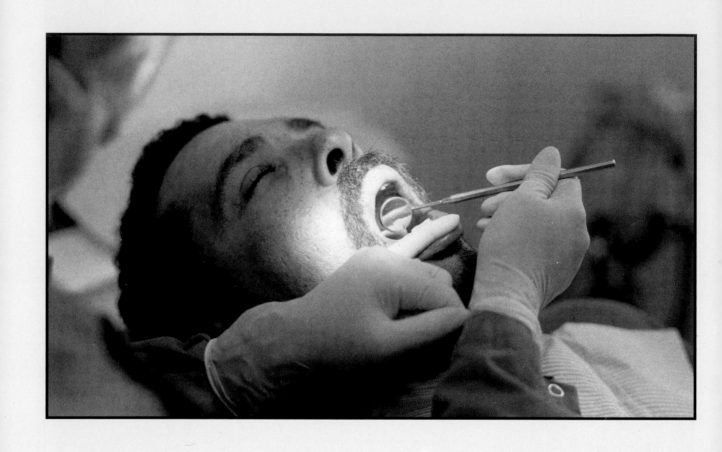

Whenever he works, he shines a bright light on our teeth.

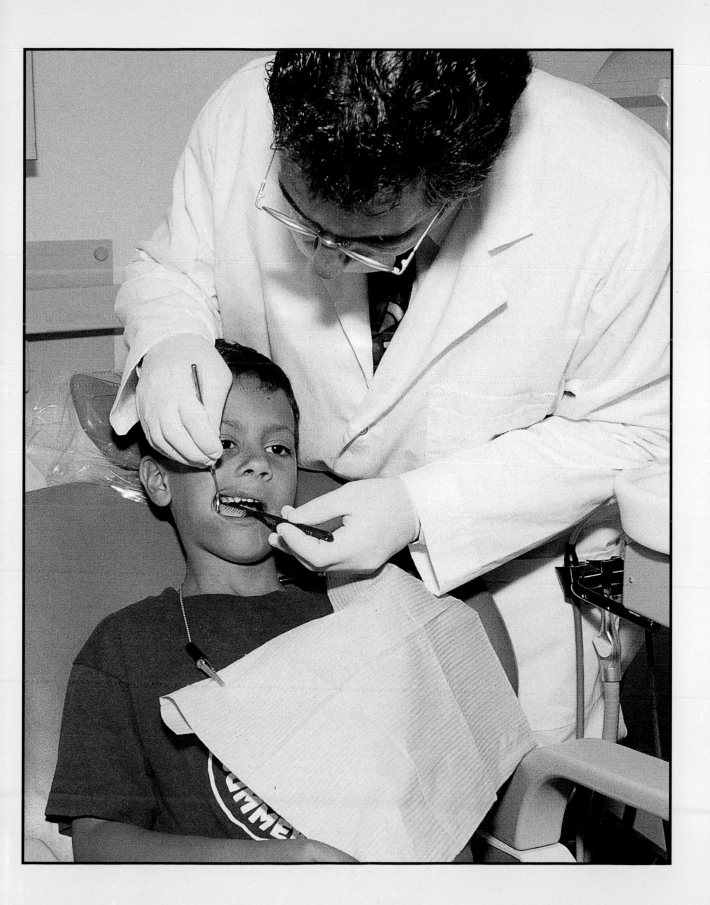

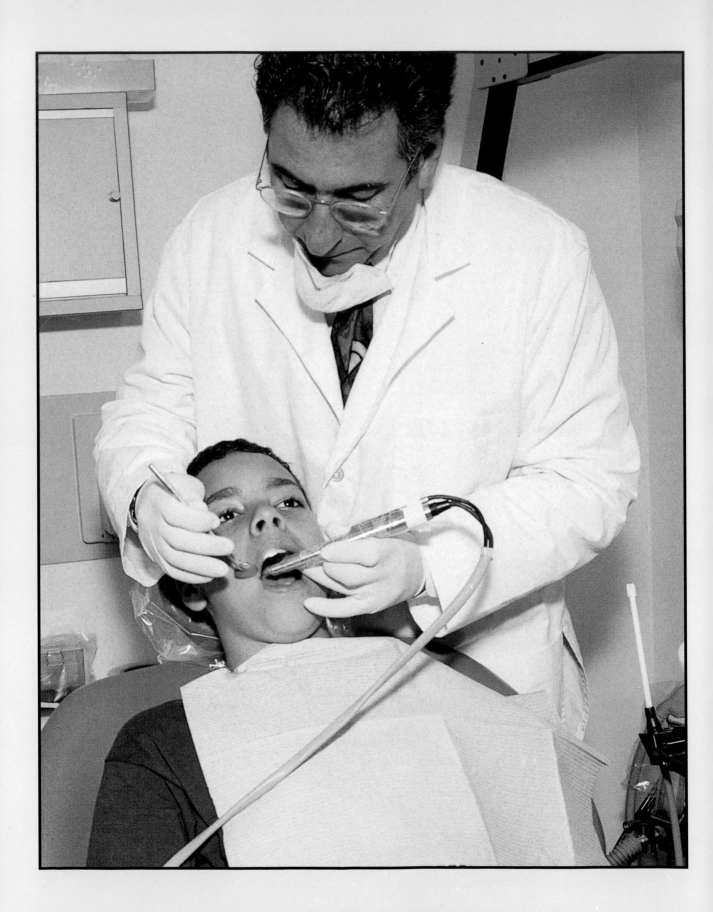

Twice a year, Dr. Kanner cleans our teeth. He checks for tooth decay, called cavities.

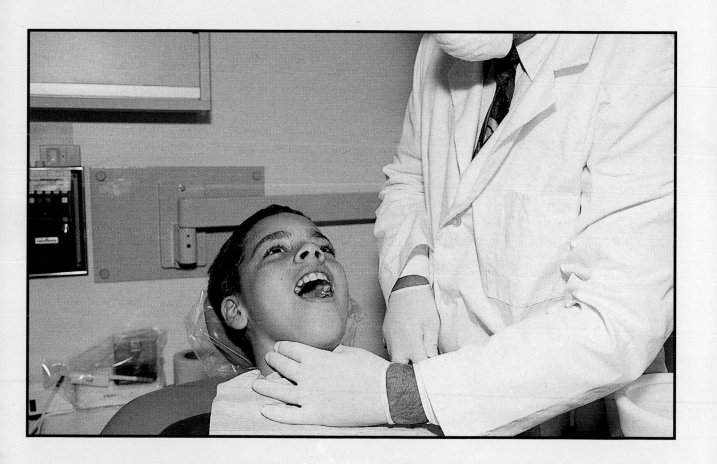

He also looks for teeth that have grown in the wrong way.

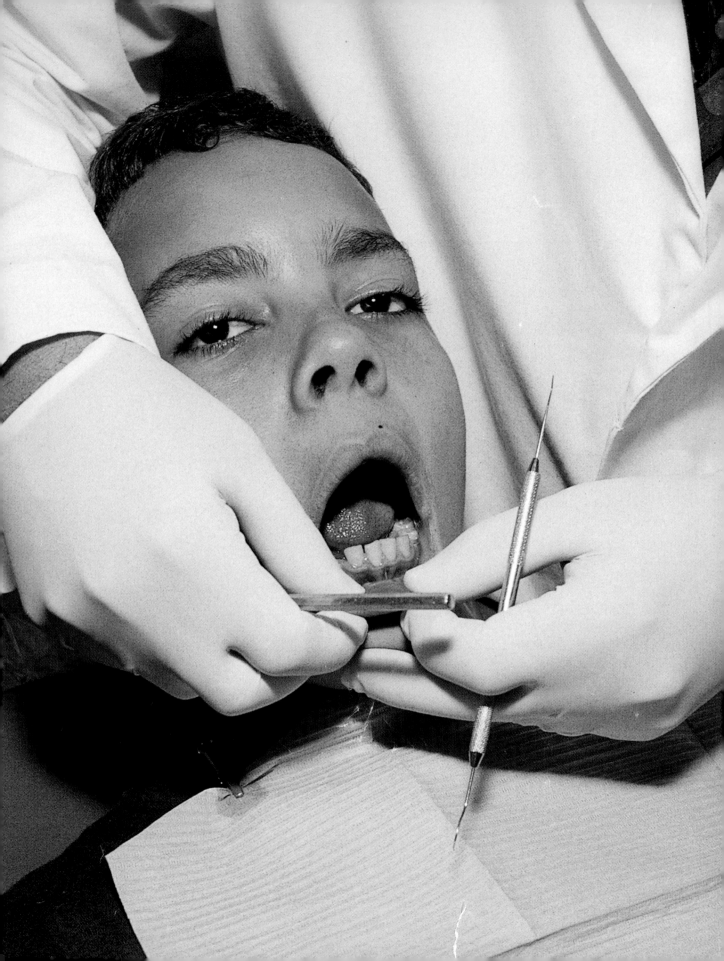

He counts our teeth and keeps a record of every one.

He uses special instruments,

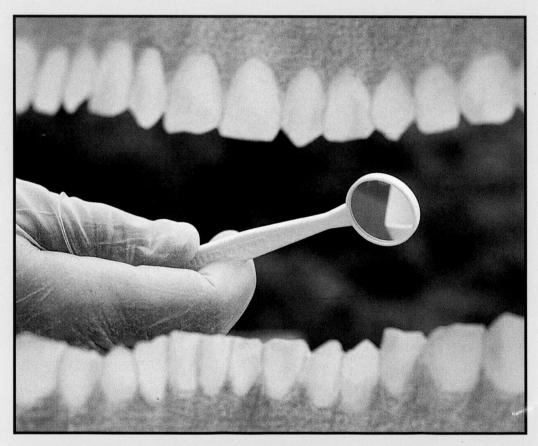

such as a tiny mirror,

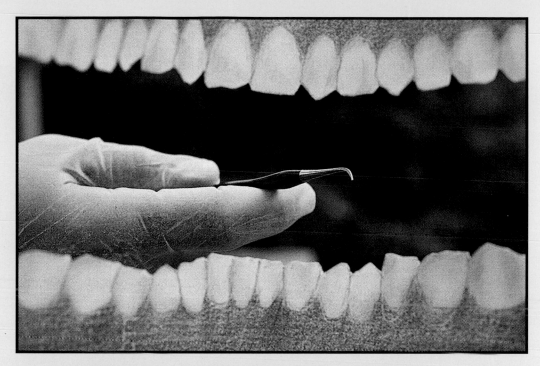

an object called an explorer,

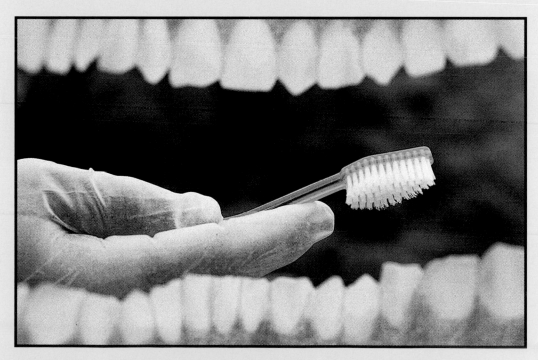

and a toothbrush.

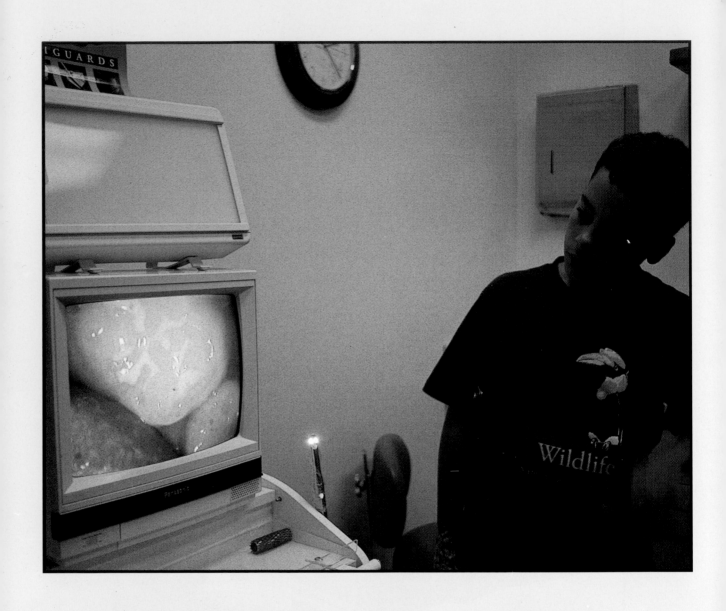

Sometimes, Dr. Kanner shows us a large picture of our teeth.

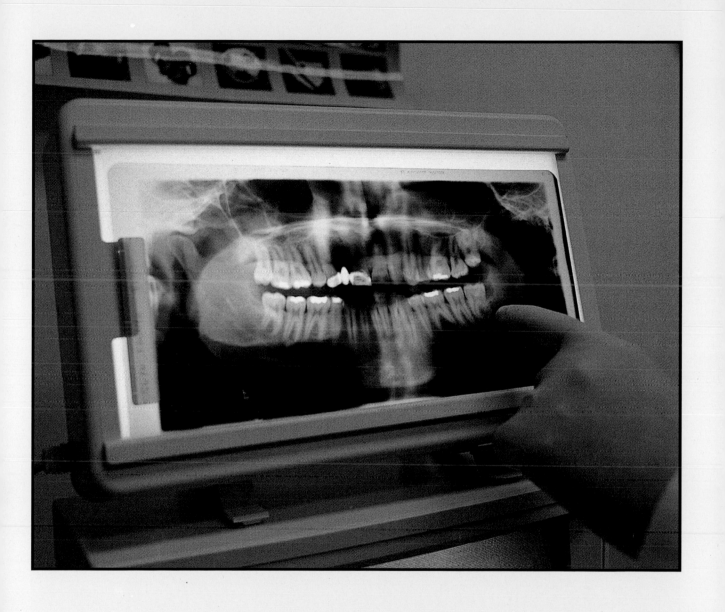

Sometimes, he X-rays our teeth so he can see the parts that are hidden by the gums.

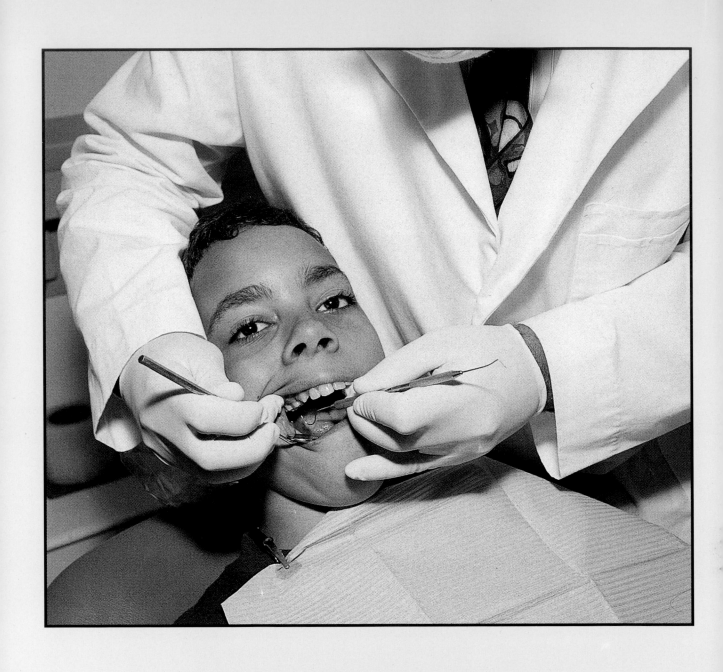

When there are cavities, Dr. Kanner
fixes them.

He asks an orthodontist to fit
special wire braces on our teeth to
straighten them.

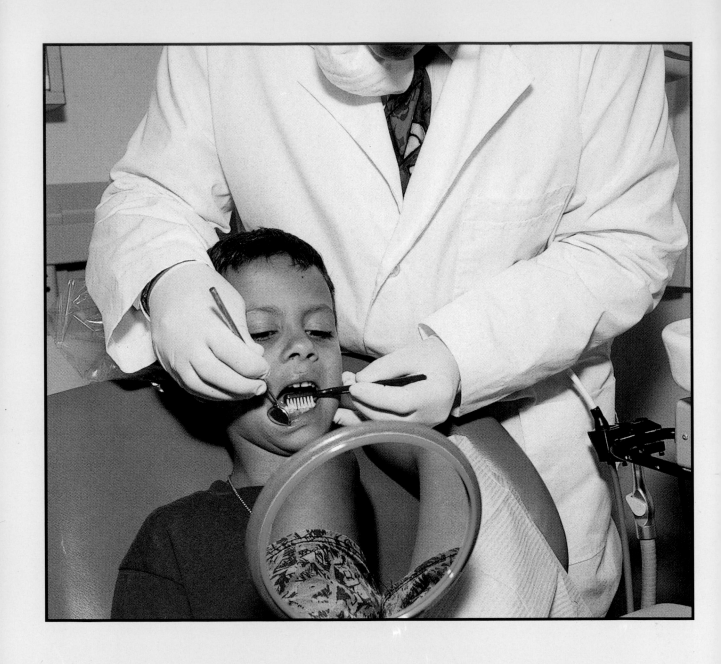

On our regular visits to Dr. Kanner's office, we learn the best way to brush our teeth.

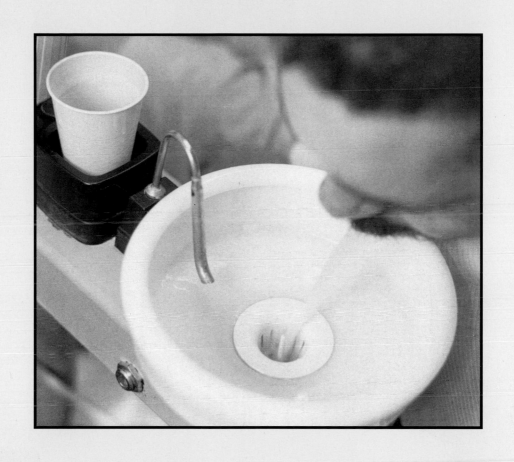

We also learn how to floss and rinse.

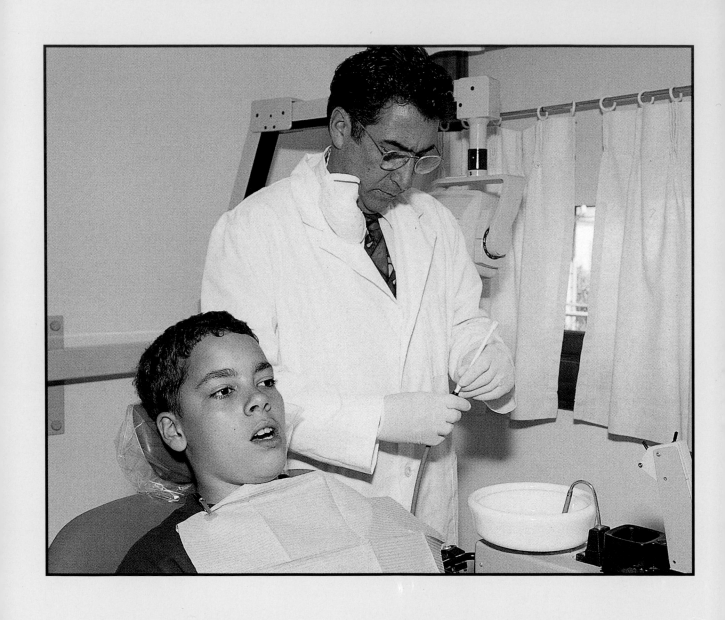

Dr. Kanner works well with
his hands.

His eyesight
must be good.

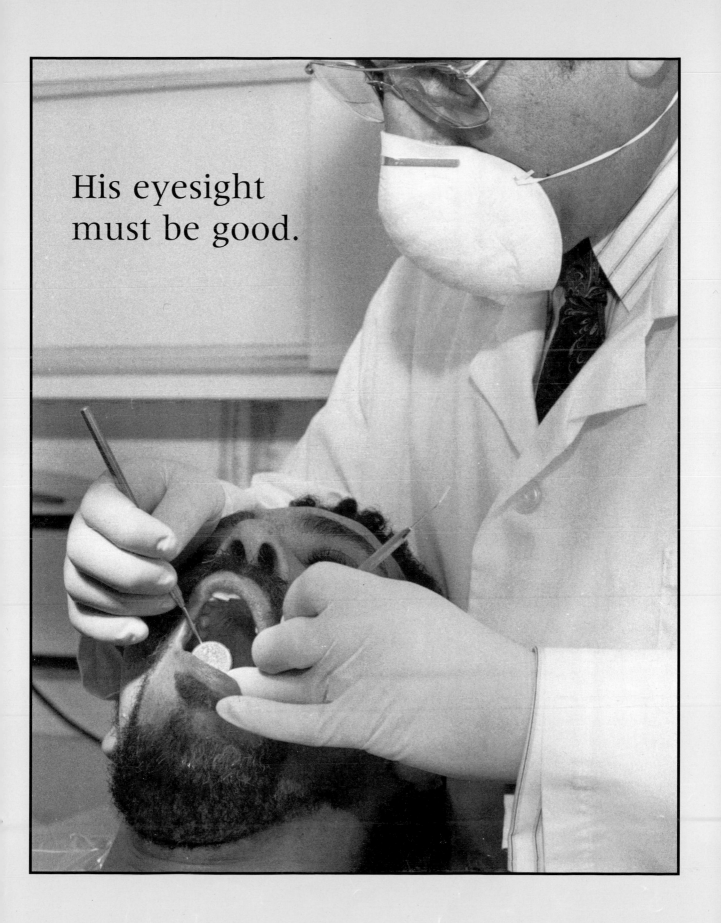

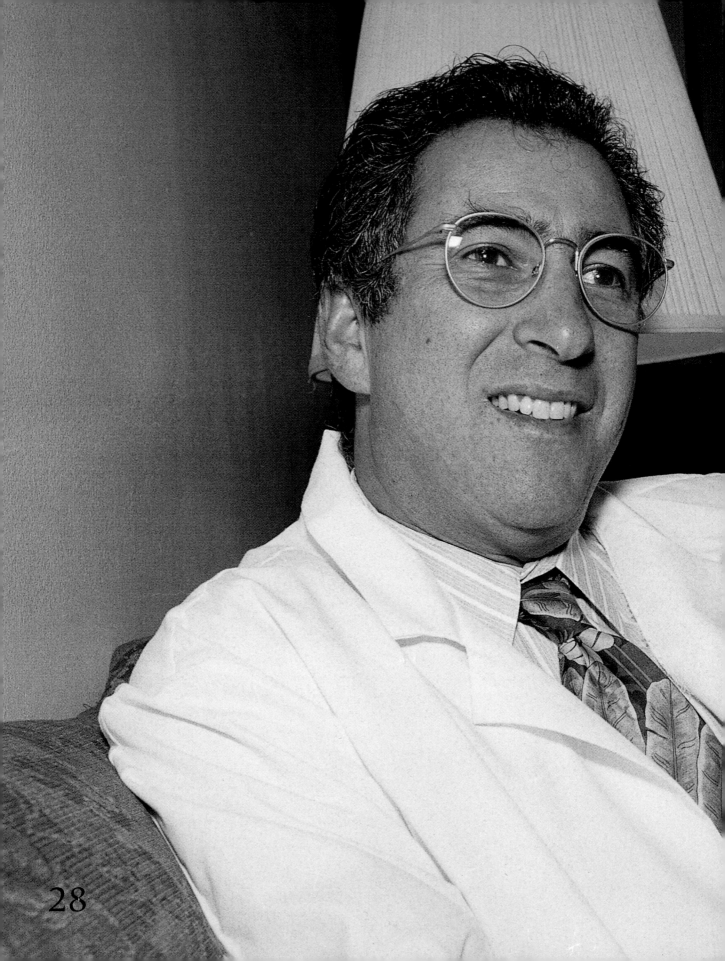

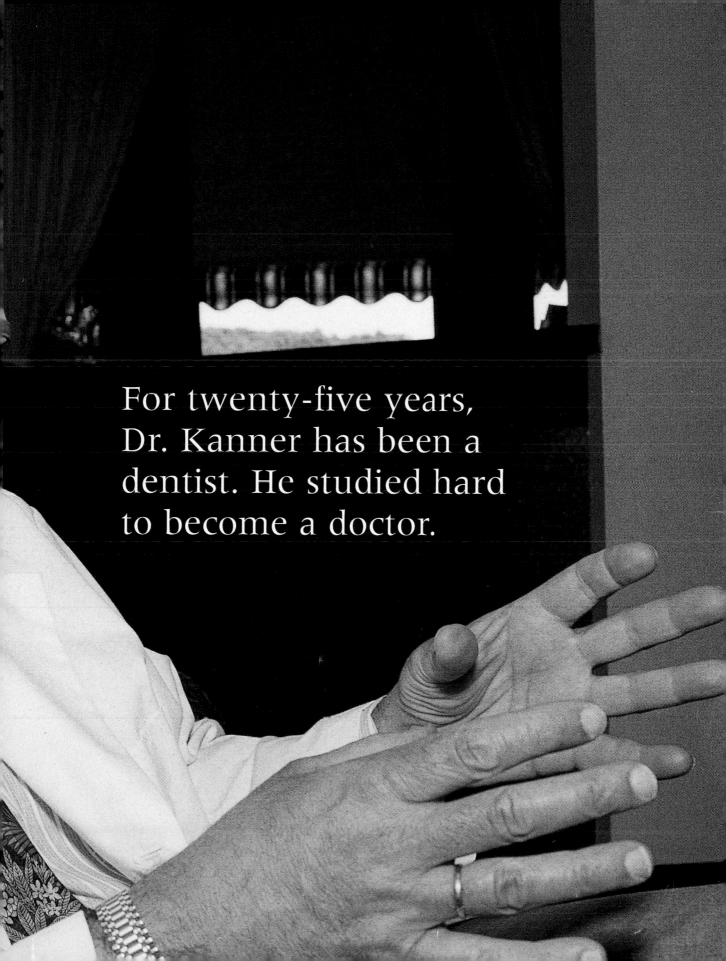

For twenty-five years,
Dr. Kanner has been a
dentist. He studied hard
to become a doctor.

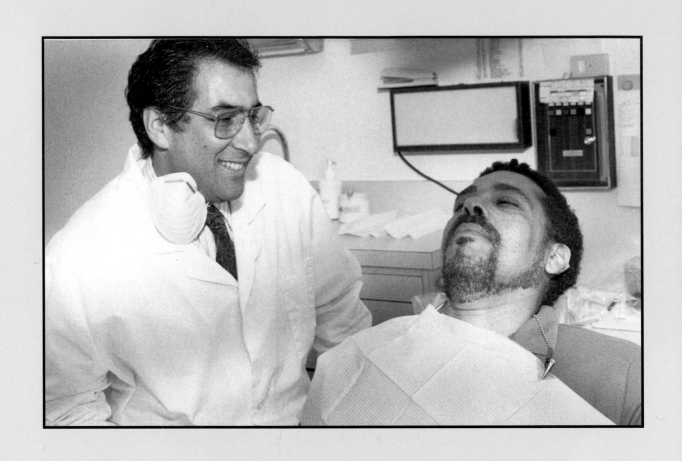

Now he cares for us.

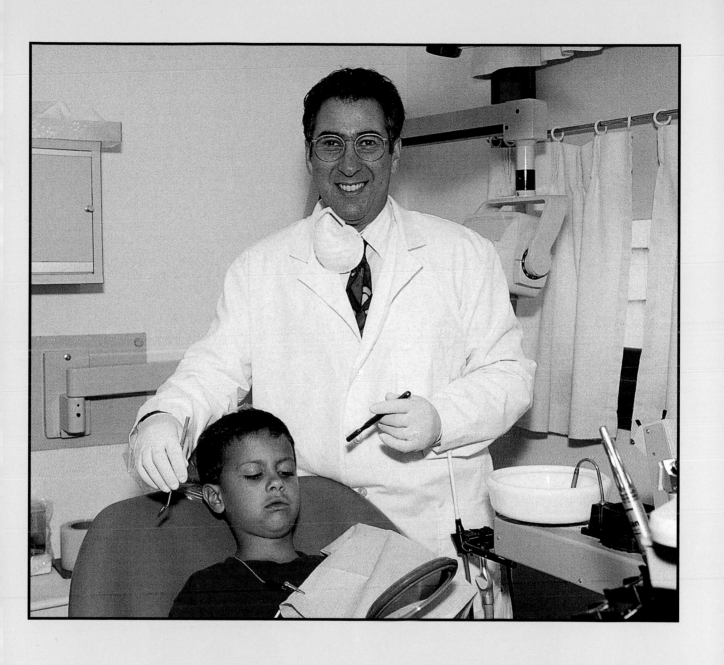

He does his best to keep our teeth healthy for the rest of our lives.

Meet the Author
and the Photographer

Alice Flanagan and Christine Osinski are sisters. They grew up together telling stories and drawing pictures in a brown brick bungalow in a southwest-side neighborhood of Chicago, Illinois. Today they write stories and take photographs professionally.

Ms. Flanagan resides in Chicago with her husband and works as a freelance writer. Ms. Osinski is a photographer and teaches at The Cooper Union for the Advancement of Science and Art in New York City. She lives with her husband and two sons on Staten Island.